D1616964

THE
BLACK BOOK OF

SHOTS
&
SHOOTERS

• *A Drinker's Guide to the Sport of Spirits* •

ERIC FURMAN AND LOU HARRY

ILLUSTRATED BY KERREN BARBAS

PETER PAUPER PRESS, INC.
WHITE PLAINS, NEW YORK

FOR SHOOTER MCGAVIN,
LONG MAY HIS SHOT BE STRAIGHT

Designed by Heather Zschock

Illustrations copyright © 2005 Kerren Barbas

Copyright © 2005
Peter Pauper Press, Inc.
202 Mamaroneck Avenue
White Plains, NY 10601
All rights reserved
ISBN 978-1-59359-998-0
Printed in Hong Kong
9 8 7 6 5 4 3 2

Visit us at www.peterpauper.com

THE LITTLE BLACK BOOK OF

SHOTS &

SHOOTERS

CONTENTS

INTRODUCTION

Alcoholic drinks are like music. They help define a moment. Remember an important moment in your life and, if there was a potent potable involved, it's likely you can recall that taste as well. The beer from that warm fraternity keg. The wine on that special evening. The champagne at that wedding.

Shooters—the specific alcoholic drinks that are the subject of this book—are among the most spirited of spirits. Largely consumed in outgoing, social groups, shooters usually arrive to smiles. Rarely do you see anything but enthusiasm when a tray of shooters arrives at a table.

First things first: Let's make the distinction clear right off the bat between shooters   and shots. A shot usually refers to a small glass of a single spirit. (One and one-half ounces is the standard U.S. measurement, but don't hold us to that when it comes to recipes.) A shot of bourbon. A shot of gin. A shot of tequila. Unadorned. Pure. A smaller shot glass, coming in at just one ounce, is known as a pony.

A shot is an efficient drink delivery system in which the goal is to finish off the entire contents at once. In other words, sipping is bad form.

And that same mentality holds true for shooters. Except that, whereas shots have their simplicity, shooters have their style. True, a shooter comes in a shot glass, but it offers a complexity of ingredients and a richness of recipe that the plain old shot lacks.

A shooter requires creativity and work, measurement and balance, a wise palate and a strong stomach. Shooters can combine juices, condiments, fruit slices, milk, any number of assorted spices and . . . other alcohols. A shooter requires its maker to be a mixologist first and an aggressive drinker third, and in between he should have a catchy name for his creation.

So, do we have it straight now? A shot can be a shooter, but a shooter can't be a shot. To put it simply: a shooter is a mixed shot.

Shooters should be fun. They should be for large groups of folks. And they should have their own unique flavor—whether that flavor goes down harsh or smooth.

This book is designed to increase the pleasures of your social drinking experience—to upgrade your bar fun and to help you be a better bartender at home.

straight shooting

I drink to make other people interesting.

GEORGE JEAN NATHAN

SHOOTER ETIQUETTE

SOME BASIC TIPS FOR A MORE POSITIVE SHOOTER EXPERIENCE:

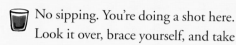 No sipping. You're doing a shot here. Look it over, brace yourself, and take it all at once.

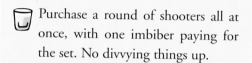 Purchase a round of shooters all at once, with one imbiber paying for the set. No divvying things up.

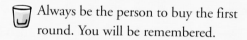 Always be the person to buy the first round. You will be remembered.

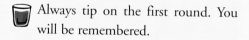 Always tip on the first round. You will be remembered.

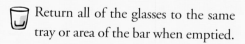 Return all of the glasses to the same tray or area of the bar when emptied.

Stacking is appreciated by many bartenders, unless it leads to a crumbling tower of broken glass.

THE BASIC SHOOTER BAR

Of course, not every shooter is consumed in a tavern. Some indulgence occurs in the privacy of one's home.

In order to maximize this pleasure, the self-tending home-owner should secure the following.

tools

GLASSWARE—The quality here depends on personal taste. For some, it's a high-end set of matching shot glasses. For others, a random assortment of souvenirs from Niagara Falls, Vegas, and various roadside attractions is perfectly acceptable. Please note: Cocktail glasses and highball glasses are acceptable, but they are not confining. In other words, if using a highball glass, you need to be careful how big a shooter you're pouring, lest you take down four ounces of 125-proof alcohol all at once (which will almost certainly do more harm than good).

Note: Clean your glassware. No one outside of a pulp novel wants a drink in a dirty glass. Keep yours clean by using suds-filled water first, then rinsing under hot water. Dry glasses upside down and have plenty on hand so that you don't have to take time out from the revelries to scrub.

SHAKERS—No, we're not talking about the uber-conservative religious groups that redefined furniture making. This is the metal gadget (don't use one that isn't metal), sizable enough not to feel like a toy, and ideally armed with an attachable slotted strainer. (Many are sold with the strainer.)

STRAINERS—Usually part of a shaker, but
 having a free-standing one is a better move. Look for small holes to insure less pulp and ice chips. Also can sub as a pretend microphone

for impromptu bar sing-a-longs.

BOTTLE OPENER—Having one handy will reduce your dental bills.

PARING KNIVES—Mostly for the fruity con-coctions.

TRAY—Nothing turns fun to flop like the bartender who tries to hand-deliver six shooters and winds up with a mess.

edibles and drinkables

- Bitters
- Bloody Mary mix
- Club soda
- Cola
- Cranberry juice
- Ginger Ale
- Grapefruit juice
- Grenadine
- Lemon-Lime soda
- Lemons
- Orange juice
- Piña Colada mix
- Pineapple juice
- Sour mix
- Tabasco sauce
- Tomato juice
- Tonic
- Worcestershire sauce

FLAME SAFETY:
A SHOOTERS SURVIVAL KIT

 There are, of course, risks to this pastime greater than just the possibility of your waking up with a throbbing hangover and/or a tattoo. To reduce these risks, heed the following:

There's primal fun in making—and downing—a flaming drink. But before you try any pyrotechnics, remember that one of the unstated goals of a shot-filled evening is to wake up the next morning without scar tissue.

To that end, put safety first—or at least in the top five.

First, forgive us for stating the obvious, but sometimes the obvious must be stated: Blow the fire out before you drink. And don't leave the drink unattended.

Other tips:

 Beware of the blue flame. No, that's not a Marvel superhero. It's what happens when you ignite alcohol. Because of the nature of the flame, you might not be able to see it under normal lighting conditions. That means don't dip your finger in for a swirl.

 Make sure the alcohol bottle is closed before you light the drink. Nobody wants an inferno.

 When selecting a glass, go for the one with the larger drink surface area. In other words, a standard shot glass is better than a test tube.

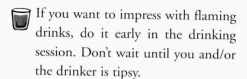 If you want to impress with flaming drinks, do it early in the drinking session. Don't wait until you and/or the drinker is tipsy.

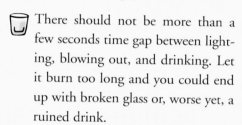 There should not be more than a few seconds time gap between lighting, blowing out, and drinking. Let it burn too long and you could end up with broken glass or, worse yet, a ruined drink.

DRIVERS: PROCEED WITH CAUTION

Let's be honest here. One of the big reasons why many people drink—particularly shooters—is to get inebriated. There's nothing wrong with that, and adults in this country are free to do so.

The problems come in what you can and can't do once you are drunk. Topping that list is driving a motor vehicle. How many drinks can you have and still drive? Rephrase the question this way: If your parent, child, or significant other were walking down the side of a highway, how many drinks would you like the drivers on the road to have had?

So err on the side of extreme caution, assign a designated driver, and consider the following:

 In many states a blood alcohol concentration as low as 0.08 while driving can carry a criminal penalty.

 Depending on various factors, (i.e. gender, weight) a 0.08 level can be reached even after only one drink.

 A "drink" is generally defined as the following: 1/2 ounce of pure alcohol (100% alcohol), which equals 1-1/4 ounces of 80-proof liquor (40% alcohol); 4 ounces of wine (12.5% alcohol); or 12 ounces of beer (4% alcohol).

 Bit of wisdom:
It's just not worth it.

recipes

Let there be dancing in the streets, drinking in the saloons, and necking in the parlor.

GROUCHO MARX,
as spoken in *A Night at the Opera*

Now, it's time to get pouring. We've selected some of the classic shooter drink recipes and combined those with interesting originals. The nature of the bar business is that creative mixers tinker with the formulas. This we encourage—just try it first before you victimize your friends.

A few things to note in these recipes: For starters, it's hard to predict how many folks you might need to create a shooter for. As we said before, shooters are best enjoyed in groups, and you never know just how big your group'll be. This makes it hard to instruct on measurements for the following recipes. So, in order to make things consistent, we keep everything in parts.

In other words, if you're making a shooter for one and it calls for two parts gin and one part juice, mentally break the glass into three parts and pour the liquids accordingly.

Also, we keep liquors and mixers generic as much as possible, but we are specific with brand names where we believe it matters. You should do the same. Trust us.

Oh, and one more thing: Remember, bartending is a combination oral/written tradition. Therefore, two different bartenders may have the same name for different drinks. For example, in our research, we found Sledgehammers made with equal parts Jack Daniel's/Tequila gold/vodka, but also with peppermint schnapps and Jägermeister, and even with J.D./Southern Comfort/sambuca. That can get confusing. But that's why we're here: to shed a little light on things and be a base for your shooter knowledge. And to help you dazzle all your friends.

brandy
shooters

Claret is the liquor for boys;
port for men; but he who aspires to
be a hero must drink brandy.

SAMUEL JOHNSON,
in James Boswell's biography
The Life of Samuel Johnson

Before you shoot these, know this:

Brandy is made from fruit juice or fruit pulp and skin. The word for this spirit comes from the Dutch word *brandewijn,* which itself means "burnt wine." Makes sense, since the Dutch traders who introduced it to their buddies in the sixteenth century tried to describe the tasty—and strong—drink they had been exposed to in Spain and Southern France as "burnt"—or "boiled"—in order to distill it. Apparently, the spirit itself goes back even further than the word, to alchemists of the seventh and eighth centuries, in the Muslim world, who experimented with distilling grapes and other fruits for medicinal purposes.

There are really three different kinds of brandies:

Grape brandy, not surprisingly, has as its root fermented grape juice. It can also be distilled from crushed, but—and this is important—*not* pressed grape pulp and skin.

Pomace brandy is made from the pressed grape pulp, skins, and stems that are left over after the grapes are squeezed to their fullest to produce juice for wine. Common examples available in the United States are grappa from Italy and marc from France. These brandies come with a bit of a punch—they're strong, but can also have an appealing fruity flavor.

Fruit brandy is pretty self-explanatory: It's the brandy that is made from fermenting fruit—except grapes. In your own recipes though, just be on the lookout for *fruit-fla-**vored* brandy. It's not the same as *fruit brandy*, but is actually just a product that comes from using other fruit-flavorings (i.e. blackberry brandy), and adding them to grape brandy.

As far as familiar brandies go, cognac is the best-known type in the world—so named because it comes from the grapes of the Cognac region of France.  Calvados, an apple brandy, comes from Normandy, one region of France that does not produce enough grapes for wine-making. France also produces a popular raspberry brandy known as Framboise. And, confusingly, sloe gin is actually a brandy—it's made from blackthorn (sloe) plums and is red in color. (You'll find shooter recipes containing sloe gin in this section of the book.)

Brandy is an agricultural spirit. It is produced when grapes and other fruits are harvested—since they cannot be stored the way grain can for making whiskey, vodka, and gin (grain spirits—get it?). Why do you need to know brandy is an agricultural spirit? Well . . . because it's helpful in determining what to mix it with, as far as shooters are concerned.

Because of its agricultural-ness, brandy has fruity flavors, so you might want to think twice before mixing it with, for example, Tabasco sauce. So, if you are creating your own shots, consider fruit juices and other sweet things (like grenadine) for your mixers.

ADAM AND EVE

1 part brandy
1 part gin
1 part Passoā Forbidden Fruit liqueur
1 splash lemon juice

Pour ingredients into shaker with crushed ice. Shake well. Strain into shot glass(es).

BRANDY-O

1 part brandy
1 splash grenadine
2 parts orange juice

Pour ingredients into shaker with crushed ice. Shake well. Strain into shot glass(es).

BULL'S SWEAT

1 part sloe gin
1 part Tabasco sauce

Pour ingredients into shaker with crushed ice. Shake well. Strain into shot glass(es).

CLIFFHANGER

1 part brandy
1 part Bailey's Irish Cream
1 part Kahlúa
Whipped cream

Pour ingredients into shaker with crushed ice. Shake well. Strain into shot glass(es).

COLORADO CIDER

1 part brandy
1 part apple schnapps
1 part cinnamon schnapps
1 splash apple juice

Pour ingredients into shaker with crushed ice. Shake well. Strain into shot glass(es).

CORPSE REVIVER

2 parts brandy
1 part Calvados apple brandy
1 part sweet vermouth

Pour directly into shot glass(es).

COUGH DROP

1 part brandy
1 part peppermint schnapps

Pour directly into shot glass(es).

LUCKY STUD

1 part Metaxa brandy
1 part Galliano liqueur

Pour ingredients into shaker with crushed ice. Shake well. Strain into shot glass(es).

MACH 1

1 part sloe gin
1 part 7-Up

Pour directly into shot glass(es).

NITRO

1 part brandy
1 part Goldschläger
1 part sambuca

Pour directly into shot glass(es).

PATRIOTIC BLOW

1 part sloe gin
1 part blue curaçao
1 squirt whipped cream

Pour sloe gin (red in color) into shot glass. Pour blue curaçao on top of it. Finish with whipped cream. Do not mix layers.

SATIN SHEET

2 parts brandy
1 splash grenadine
1 part peach schnapps
4 parts orange juice

Pour ingredients into shaker with crushed ice. Shake well. Strain into shot glass(es).

gin
shooters

*Let's all drink gin and
make wry faces.*

BOB HOPE
in *The Cat and the Canary*

Before you shoot these, know this:

The name "gin" is the English shortening of the Dutch word *genever*, which means juniper. Gin's earliest roots can be traced back to seven-teenth century Holland, where it was used as medicine for stomach complaints, gall-stones, and gout. The British took some ownership of the liquor when, during the Thirty Years' War, the King's troops were given "Dutch Courage" to erase—er, ease—their minds. They brought it home with them to their families and their home-towns. Today, good gin makers can be found wherever there are British and Dutch influences—the USA, Australia, and New Zealand, for example.

Gin is a grain spirit. It is made by first distilling a neutral grain, and then throwing in botanicals for the next round of distilling. These botanicals usually include juniper berries, but may also include anise, coriander, lime, lemon and orange peel, licorice, bitter almonds, caraway seeds, cardamom, and angelica root.

There are a few key varieties of gin:

English or London Dry Gin is the most mixable gin, primarily because it comes from a grain or molasses that usually doesn't have much flavor.

Dutch/Genever/Sweet/Holland Gin has a flavor that comes mainly from juniper berries and cereal grains—hence the "sweet" in its name. This gin, because of its unique flavor, is not generally considered to be much of a mixer, and most bartenders recommend it on the rocks. So get ready to pucker up!

American Dry Gin is lower in proof and less flavorful than London Dry Gin. It is, however, easily mixable, especially when it's all you've got.

Because gin is a grain alcohol *and* it has as its main flavor characteristic a fruity, fresh taste, you have to be careful what you mix it with. We recommend other sweet, fruity flavors. Anything with a licorice aftertaste is okay, such as grape juice, lime juice, blue curaçao, and the like. Stay away from milk and dairy, in general.

One final note: Many people recommend that you drink gin straight, over ice in a highball glass or stirred with ice and strained into a martini glass. We'll agree with them, in principle, but suggest the (mixed) shooters that follow.

Please remember, slice gin is not really gin. Your shots will taste funny if you pour sloe gin when the recipe calls for dry gin. (Just keepin' you on your toes.)

BLACKOUT

2 parts gin
2 parts blackberry brandy
1 part lime juice
1 part sugar syrup

Pour ingredients into shaker with crushed ice. Shake well. Strain into shot glass(es).

DEVASTATING BODY ROCKER

1 part gin
1 part blackberry brandy

Pour directly into shot glass(es).

EMERALD EYE

1 part gin
1 part blue curaçao
1 part Midori melon liqueur

Pour directly into shot glass(es).

EVIL TONGUE

2 parts gin
1 part Midori melon liqueur
1 splash sour mix
1 splash 7-Up

Pour ingredients into shaker with crushed ice. Shake well. Strain into shot glass(es).

GIN AND BEAR IT

1 part gin
1/2 part beer

Mix and shoot!

GIN AND FRESCA

1 part gin
1 part Fresca

No mystery here. Mix these two ingredients into shot glass(es) and drink.

GIN DAISY

2 parts gin
1 part lemon juice
1 teaspoon sugar
1 splash grenadine

Pour ingredients into shaker with crushed ice. Shake well. Strain into shot glass(es).

HONOLULU

1 part gin
1 splash lemon juice
1 splash orange juice
1 splash pineapple juice
1 splash pineapple syrup
1 drop Angostura bitters

Mix all ingredients in a shaker with ice. Strain into shot glass(es) and serve.

ITALIAN VALIUM

1 part gin
2 parts amaretto

Pour ingredients into shaker with crushed ice. Shake well. Strain into shot glass(es).

PAMOYO

1 part gin
1 part grape juice
1 part Sprite

Pour ingredients into shaker with crushed ice. Shake well. Strain into shot glass(es).

PATAGONIAN BLACK BUSH

2 parts gin
1 part Fernet-Branca
1 dash sour mix

Pour directly into shot glass(es).

PINK GIN

1 part dry gin
1 splash cranberry juice

Pour directly into shot glass(es).

PLEAD THE 5TH

1 part gin
1 part Kahlúa
1 part sambuca

Pour ingredients into shaker with crushed ice. Shake well. Strain into shot glass(es).

SLINGSHOT

1 part gin
1 part peach schnapps
1 part sour mix
1 dash grenadine

Pour ingredients into shaker over ice and strain into shot glass(es).

rum
shooters

*There's nought, no doubt, so
much the spirit calms
as rum and true religion.*

LORD BYRON, *Don Juan*

Before you shoot these, know this:

 Sugar and water. These are the main ingredients in rum. In other words, it's sweet stuff. Rum was discovered when sugar mill operators in the Caribbean noticed that the leftover molasses they produced, when mixed with water and left out in the sun, would ferment. The English colonials called the spirit Kill Devil (because it caused quite a hangover) and rumbullion (the origin of which is unclear). Obviously, the second term is the longer version of our favorite sweet, hard liquor.

Rum has its own set of classifications.

White Rums are so named because of their light-bodied-ness and clear color. Their complex taste is worthy of a connoisseur's palate. White rums blend well with almost all fruit flavors.

Golden, or Amber, Rums are medium-bodied.

Dark Rums exhibit a heady caramel flavor. They are mostly full-bodied, and aged in casks for many years. They are not generally good for mixing, and tend to be drunk straight up.

Spiced Rums can be white, golden, or dark, and exhibit spice (duh) and fruit flavors.

Rum grew out of tropical island locales, but now rivals vodka as the mixer of choice in a whole slew of non-tropical places. It is produced in every region of the world, on every continent except Antarctica. Perhaps this is due to its high sugar content (sweet things, as we here in America know, are always extremely appealing). Rum mixes well with many things—it balances out the not-so-sweet stuff and intensifies the really

sweet treats. In other words, if Tabasco sauce is to your liking, Bacardi 151-proof rum will go just fine with it; and if peach schnapps is more your speed, you can feel free to mix it with some white rum. Chocolate, banana, dry vermouth . . . all are acceptable when it comes to rum shooters.

BLUE SMURF PISS

1 part Bacardi 151-proof rum
1 part blue curaçao
1 part Goldschläger
1 part Jägermeister
1 part Rumple Minze

Pour ingredients into shaker with crushed ice. Shake well. Strain into shot glass(es).

BUTTERNUT RUM LIFESAVER

1 part rum
1 part Bailey's Irish Cream
1 part butterscotch schnapps
1 part pineapple juice

Pour ingredients into shaker with crushed ice. Shake well. Strain into shot glass(es).

CORKSCREW

2 parts light rum
1 part dry vermouth
1 part peach schnapps
1 lemon slice

Pour ingredients into shaker with crushed ice. Shake well. Strain into shot glass(es). After taking shot, suck on lemon.

FIERY NIPPLE

1 part butterscotch schnapps
1 part Bailey's Irish Cream
1 part Goldschläger
1 dash Bacardi 151-proof rum

In shot glass(es), float each ingredient over the previous. Set on fire. Blow out. Shoot.

FLAMING GIRAFFE

2 parts Kahlúa
1 part butterscotch schnapps
1 part Bacardi 151-proof rum

Pour Kahlúa into shot glass(es). Add schnapps. Float Bacardi 151 on top. Set on fire. Be sure to blow it out before drinking.

THE GRINCH

1 part rum
1 part banana liqueur
1 part Midori melon liqueur
1 splash 7-Up

Pour ingredients into shaker with crushed ice. Shake well. Strain into shot glass(es).

LIQUID COCAINE

1 part Bacardi 151-proof rum
1 part Goldschläger
1 part Jägermeister

Pour ingredients directly into shot glass(es).

ORANGE CRISIS

2 parts light rum
2 parts peach schnapps
1 part apricot brandy
1 part triple sec
1 part cream
1 splash grenadine

Pour ingredients into shaker with crushed ice. Shake well. Strain into shot glass(es).

RUMKA

1 part rum
1 part vodka

Pour ingredients into shaker with crushed ice. Shake well. Strain into shot glass(es).

SCOOBY SNACK

1 part rum
1 part crème de bananes
1 part Midori melon liqueur
1 part pineapple juice
1 part whipped cream

Pour ingredients (including whipped cream) into shaker with crushed ice. Shake well. Strain into shot glass(es).

SPARKPLUG

1 part Bacardi 151-proof rum
1 part Rumple Minze

Pour Bacardi 151 directly into glass(es). Add Rumple Minze. Do not mix.

SUICIDE: THE SHOT

6 parts Bacardi 151-proof rum
1 part Tabasco sauce

Pour rum directly into shot glass(es). Float Tabasco on top of rum. Do not stir.

SURFER ON ACID

1 part rum
1 part Jägermeister
1 part pineapple juice

Pour ingredients into shaker with crushed ice. Shake well. Strain into shot glass(es).

TWIN SISTERS

1 part Bacardi light rum
1 part Bacardi spiced rum
1 dash cola
1 dash lime juice

Pour ingredients into shaker with crushed ice. Shake well. Strain into shot glass(es).

tequila
shooters

*A computer lets you make more
mistakes faster than any invention
in human history—with the possible
exceptions of handguns and tequila.*

MITCH RATCLIFFE,
Technology Review (April, 1992)

Before you shoot these, know this:

Tequila was originally produced by religious authorities in Mexico; that's right—the spiritual advisors made the spirits. The product wasn't known as tequila at that time, but as Mezcal wine, named for the plant from which its main ingredient was drawn. Then, in 1656, the Spanish discovered the town of Tequila, in a valley in the Jalisco state, and soon realized that the town was convenient to the also newly-established port of San Blas.

One man saw opportunity in Tequila, and in 1758 he became the first to be licensed to cultivate and manufacture "tequila." That gentleman's name: Jose Antonio Cuervo. Señor Cuervo grew agave plants on his land, and made his tequila from agave instead of mezcal. By the middle of the nineteenth century he had plantations containing more than three million of those plants.

There are differences between mezcal and tequila, both in process and in taste. For a liquor to be truly a tequila, at least 51 percent of it must be made from the agave plant. While tequila is always double- and sometimes triple-distilled, Mezcal is generally distilled only once. Mezcals are a little stronger, but they are also harsher to the taste. Consequently, we currently can find over 500 different brands of tequila, while there exist only about 100 brands of mezcal.

The worm (a butterfly caterpillar) is not, as is commonly thought, a traditional inhabitant of the tequila bottle. Originally, the worms were sometimes accidentally left over in bottles of mezcal or tequila; now, canny producers add it as a come-on. "Hey, get a worm free with every bottle of tequila!" And, in case you are interested and have a subtle palate, know that the red worm is considered superior to the white worm (that turns gray in the liquid). It's OK to eat the worm if you are lucky enough to find it in your glass. After all, it's mostly protein and alcohol, and it won't hurt you! Down the hatch!

When creating your own tequila shooters, keep in mind that mezcal and agave are plants. Again, just like with brandy, we're talking about an agricultural liquor. So stay away from milk and dairy-like products. However, because tequila has a fiery flavor, it mixes well with spicy things like Tabasco sauce and ... oh, say, Hot Tamales candies. Not that we're admitting we tried that; it's just a thought.

ARMY GREEN

1 part tequila
1 part Goldschläger
1 part Jägermeister

Pour directly into shot glass(es).

BLACK CACTUS

1 part tequila
1 part blackberry brandy
1 part club soda

Pour ingredients into shaker with crushed ice. Shake well. Strain into shot glass(es).

CAPTAIN CRUNCH

1 part Tequila Rose
1 part Kahlúa
1 part vanilla schnapps
1 part cream
1 splash grenadine

Pour ingredients into shaker with crushed ice. Shake well. Strain into shot glass(es).

DEEP BLUE SEA

2 parts tequila
1 part blue curaçao

Pour tequila into shot glass(es). Then, carefully, slowly pour blue curaçao down side of glass so that it rests under the tequila. Do not mix.

DIRTY SAILOR

1 part tequila
1 squeeze mayonnaise

Pour tequila directly into glass(es). Squeeze small portion of mayonnaise from disposable packet into shot.

FLAT TIRE

2 parts Jose Cuervo Especial Gold Tequila
1 part black sambuca

Pour ingredients into shaker with crushed ice. Shake well. Strain into shot glass(es).

FLATLINER

1 part sambuca
1-1/2 parts tequila
3 dashes Tabasco sauce

In a shot glass, first pour the sambuca. Then add the tequila. Finally, add the dashes of Tabasco sauce. Keep layers. Do not mix.

GRATEFUL DEAD

1 part tequila
1 part rum
1 part vodka
1 part Chambord
1 part triple sec

Pour ingredients into shaker with crushed ice. Shake well. Strain into shot glass(es).

LUMBERJACK

1 part tequila
1 part ouzo
1 part sambuca
1 dash Tabasco sauce

Pour alcohols directly into shot glass(es). Add dash of hot sauce.

MEXICAN PRAIRIE FIRE

3 parts Jose Cuervo Especial Gold Tequila
1 part Tabasco sauce

Pour tequila directly into shot glass(es). Float Tabasco on top of tequila. Do not stir.

THE MUPPET

1 part tequila
1 part 7-Up

Pour liquids directly into shot glass(es). Place palm over top of glass, lift and slam on table to mix. Then shoot immediately.

ROOSTER TAIL

1 shot Jose Cuervo Especial Gold Tequila
1 shot orange juice
1 shot tomato juice
1 dash salt

 Pour Jose Cuervo, orange juice, and tomato juice into separate shot glasses. Lick top of hand. Pour salt on licked area. When ready, quickly lick salt off of hand and down (in order) tequila, orange juice, and tomato juice.

SPIDER BITE

1 part tequila
1 part anisette

Pour ingredients into shaker with crushed ice. Shake well. Strain into shot glass(es).

T.K.O.

1 part tequila
1 part Kahlúa
1 part ouzo

Pour ingredients into shaker with crushed ice. Shake well. Strain into shot glass(es).

TEQUILA SUNSET

2 parts tequila
2 parts orange juice
1 part blackberry brandy
1 maraschino cherry

Pour tequila and orange juice into shaker with crushed ice. Shake well. Pour into shot glass(es). Add brandy. Drink. Eat cherry.

THREE SHEETS TO THE WIND

1 part tequila
1 part Jägermeister
1 part Rumple Minze

Pour directly into shot glass(es).

WHITE TORNADO

3 parts sambuca
1 part Tequila Rose

Pour sambuca directly into shot glass(es).
Then pour Tequila Rose slowly down side of
shot glass and spin the glass.

vodka
shooters

*And you don't drink the vodka
down right away. No, sir. First you
take a deep breath, wipe your hands,
and glance up at the ceiling to
demonstrate your indifference. Only
then do you raise that vodka slowly
to your lips and suddenly…sparks!
They fly from your stomach to the
farthest reaches of your body.*

ANTON CHEKHOV, *The Siren*

Before you shoot these, know this:

Vodka is widely considered the most popular mixer in the world. It was first produced in Poland or Russia or both, and inhabitants of the two countries have a long history of drinking the stuff like water. Interestingly enough, the Russian word *voda*, assumed to be the origin of vodka, means "water." Interchangeable in Russia, no?

This clean spirit was used for medicinal purposes—as an anesthetic and disinfectant distilled from rye—as early as the twelfth century. Although vodka's beginnings were in rye, it soon became a potato-based spirit, for it was much cheaper to produce and easier to distill.  Soon, however, because the vodka simply didn't taste as good when being mass produced, the switch was made to corn, wheat, rye, and barley. Today, vodka is distilled until it reaches a high alcoholic content, and then filtered through vegetable charcoal. This results in an extremely clear liquid that has very little flavor. This is good for us, because it makes a perfect mixer for shooters. Vodka has an ability to adapt and accentuate the flavor of almost any ingredient, from other alcohols to fruit juices to peppermint to milk. Yes, milk. It's one of the few spirits that will do all right with dairy. So . . . if you have to go out and buy one alcohol to mix a variety of shots with, make it vodka. Anything you pull out of your refrigerator or cabinet will make you seem like a creative genius. Well, unless it's two-week-old Chinese leftovers and pickle juice. That's just gross.

ANTI-FREEZE

1 part vodka
1 part crème de menthe

Pour ingredients into a shaker over ice. Shake and strain into shot glass(es).

APPLE CAKE

1 part vanilla vodka
1 part apple liqueur
1 dash cinnamon

Pour ingredients into shaker with crushed ice. Shake well. Strain into shot glass(es).

APPLE DUMPLING

4 parts vodka
2 parts cinnamon schnapps
1 part apple juice

Pour ingredients into shaker with crushed ice. Shake well. Strain into shot glass(es).

APPLE PIE

1 part vodka
1 part apple sauce

Pour vodka directly into shot glass(es). Add spoonful of apple sauce.

BLOW JOB

1 part Kahlúa
1 part Bailey's Irish Cream
1 part vodka
Whipped cream

Pour ingredients—minus whipped cream—into shaker with crushed ice. Shake well. Strain into shot glass(es). Top with whipped cream. Preferably find an attractive bar-goer to place the full shooter between his/her knees as he/she sits on a stool. Without using your hands, wrap your lips completely around the outer edge of the shot glass, lift from between the knees, tilt your head back, and chug.

BRUISED HEART

1 part vodka
1 part Chambord
1 part peach schnapps
1 part cranberry juice

Pour ingredients into shaker with crushed ice. Shake well. Strain into shot glass(es).

CASBA SHOT

2 parts vodka
2 parts triple sec
1 part Chambord
1 part lime juice
1 part sour mix

Pour ingredients into shaker with crushed ice. Shake well. Strain into shot glass(es).

CHOCOLATE CAKE

1 part vodka
1 part Frangelico
Sugar
Lemon slice

Pour vodka and Frangelico into shaker with crushed ice. Shake well. Strain into shot glass(es). Finish by sucking on sugar-coated lemon slice.

DEAD NAZI

1 part vodka
1 part Jägermeister
1 part Rumple Minze

Pour ingredients into shaker with crushed ice. Shake well. Strain into shot glass(es).

4TH OF JULY

1 part grenadine
1 part vodka
1 part blue curaçao

Pour into shot glass(es) in the following order: grenadine, vodka, blue curaçao.

HAWAIIAN

1 part vodka
1 part amaretto
1 part cranberry juice

Pour ingredients into shaker with crushed ice. Shake well. Strain into shot glass(es).

KAMIKAZE

4 parts vodka
3 parts triple sec
1 dash of lime juice
1 splash of sour mix

Pour ingredients into shaker with crushed ice. Shake well. Strain into shot glass(es).

KEY LIME PIE

3 parts Licor 43
1 part vodka
1 part Rose's Lime Juice
1 part milk or cream

Pour ingredients into shaker with crushed ice. Shake well. Strain into shot glass(es).

MIND ERASER

1 part Kahlúa
2 parts vodka
2 splashes butterscotch schnapps
1 splash cola

Fill a highball glass with ice. Carefully layer each liquid; start with the Kahlúa, then the vodka, then the schnapps, and finally the cola. Be careful not to mix. Using a straw, slurp the shot from bottom of the glass until it is gone. Do not sip; do not pause.

MUDSLIDE

1 part vodka
1 part Kahlúa
1 part Bailey's Irish Cream

Pour ingredients into shaker with crushed ice. Shake well. Strain into shot glass(es).

POLAR BEAR

1 part vodka
1 part peppermint schnapps

Pour ingredients into shaker with crushed ice. Shake well. Strain into shot glass(es).

PURPLE HOOTER

1 part vodka
1 part Chambord
1 splash 7-Up

Pour ingredients into shaker with crushed ice. Shake well. Strain into shot glass(es).

PURPLEPALOOZA

2 parts Bacardi Limón
1 part blue curaçao
1 part seltzer water
1 splash grenadine

Pour ingredients into shaker with crushed ice. Shake well. Strain into shot glass(es).

RED SHARK

1 part vodka
1 part bourbon
1 part amaretto
3 dashes grenadine
2 dashes hot sauce

Pour ingredients into shaker with crushed ice. Shake well. Strain into shot glass(es).

SEA BREEZE

2 parts vodka
3 parts cranberry juice
3 parts grapefruit juice

Pour ingredients into shaker with crushed ice. Shake well. Strain into shot glass(es).

SEX ON THE BEACH

1 part vodka
1 part peach schnapps
3 parts cranberry juice
3 parts orange or pineapple juice

Pour ingredients into shaker with crushed ice. Shake well. Strain into shot glass(es).

SHARPSHOOTER

1 part vodka
1 part ouzo
6 drops Tabasco sauce

Pour ingredients directly into shot glass(es).

SILK PANTIES

2 parts vodka
2 parts peach schnapps
1 part raspberry liqueur

Pour ingredients into a shaker over ice.
Shake and strain into shot glass(es).

STOPLIGHT

3 shots vodka
1 splash Midori melon liqueur
1 splash orange juice
1 splash cranberry juice

Line up three vodka shot glasses in a row. Add a splash of Midori to one, a splash of orange juice to another, and a splash of cranberry juice to the last one. Then drink them down. Green light—go! Yellow light—keep going! Red light—stop, you're all done!

THE TRIPLE

1 part vodka
1 part Goldschläger
1 part Jägermeister

Pour ingredients into shot glass(es) and serve.

whiskey and bourbon shooters

Whiskey—I like it,
I always did, and that is
the reason I never use it.

GENERAL ROBERT E. LEE

Before you shoot these, know this:

Whiskey. Bourbon. What the hell's the difference? Well, not much, except a few percentage points. See, to be labeled a bourbon, the spirit must contain at least 51 percent corn. Whiskey, on the other hand, can have higher percentages of barley malt, wheat, and rye. Whiskey's been around longer—some Irishmen claim its traditions go back 1,000 years, to the time when beer was first being created and its remnants likely distilled.

Bourbon got its name along the Ohio and Mississippi Rivers in the 1700s, when immigrant Kentucky farmers began to make the stuff from their corn. The whiskey was

 shipped down to New Orleans, from its starting point— Bourbon County, Kentucky. Pretty soon, folks started calling it "that whiskey from Bourbon," which quickly was shortened to

"bourbon." Not so unbeliev-
ably, bourbon and whiskey go
through similar distillation
processes, and many of the
same flavors can be found in
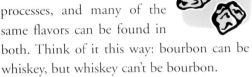
both. Think of it this way: bourbon can be
whiskey, but whiskey can't be bourbon.

Bourbon is aged for anywhere from two
to eight years. Since it improves with age,
look for that (more expensive) longer-aged
bourbon on your retailer's shelves. Also of
note: many of today's best bourbons are
stored in oak barrels that have been charred
on the inside, giving the liquor its reddish
color and smoky flavor.

Whiskeys—especially Irish and
Scotch—are considered a fine drink, with flavors to be appreciated all on their own, either
neat or on the rocks. In other words, you'll
not find a lot of Irish whiskeys or scotches
included in shooter recipes. That leaves us
with bourbon, a distinctly American product.

In fact, no other country in the world produces a whiskey called "bourbon."

So most of the following recipes will include bourbon. In some cases, because of the distinctive spices and flavors of a particular brand (for example, Southern Comfort), we suggest a specific bourbon. But in most cases, any bourbon will do.

As for creating your own shots, it's helpful to remember that bourbon mixes well with bubbly things—like cola, 7-Up and soda water. Sweeteners like grenadine, amaretto, and sour mix also will enhance your bourbon shooter experience. Also, different bourbons tend to mix well with others in shots, because the flavors and potency can be so wide-ranging. Again, as we've seen before, stay away from milk. (Are you seeing a pattern yet?)

ALABAMA SLAMMER

1 part Southern Comfort
1 part amaretto
1 part sloe gin
1 splash orange juice
1 splash sour mix

Pour ingredients into shaker with crushed ice. Shake well. Strain into shot glass(es).

THE ATP

1 part bourbon
1 part amaretto

Pour directly into shot glass(es).

BEAM ME UP

1 part Jim Beam bourbon
1 part amaretto
3 parts cola

Pour ingredients into shaker with crushed ice. Shake well. Strain into shot glass(es).

BEAM SCREAM

1 part Jim Beam bourbon
1 part Aftershock

Pour directly into shot glass(es).

BLOOD CLOT

2 parts Southern Comfort
1 part grenadine
3 parts 7-Up

Mix grenadine and 7-Up in a pint glass (approximately half-full). Drop a shot glass full of Southern Comfort into the pint. Chug.

BRAIN DAMAGE

2 parts bourbon
1 part Tía Maria coffee liqueur
2 to 3 drops grenadine

Pour directly into shot glass(es). Do not mix.

CHERRY BLOW POP

1 part bourbon
1 part amaretto
1 part grenadine

Pour ingredients into shaker with crushed ice. Shake well. Strain into shot glass(es).

CHERRY LIFESAVER

1 part bourbon
1 part amaretto
2 parts sour mix
1 splash grenadine

Pour ingredients into shaker with crushed ice. Shake well. Strain into shot glass(es).

DEPRESSED GOALIE

1-1/2 parts bourbon
1 part cola
1 part Mountain Dew

Pour ingredients into shaker with crushed ice. Shake well. Strain into shot glass(es).

FRUITY PASSION

1 part bourbon
1 part triple sec
1 part grenadine

Pour directly into shot glass(es).

GREEN APPLE

1 part bourbon
1 splash Midori melon liqueur
1 splash sour mix

Pour directly into shot glass(es).

JIM'S NUTS

1 part Jim Beam bourbon
1 part amaretto

Pour directly into shot glass(es).

KENTUCKY WILDCAT

1 part Jack Daniel's
1 part Jim Beam bourbon
1 part Southern Comfort
1 part Yukon Jack
2 parts sour mix
2 parts Coca-Cola

Pour ingredients into shaker with crushed ice. Shake well. Strain into shot glass(es).

PINEAPPLE BOMB

1 part bourbon
1 part triple sec
1 part pineapple juice
1 splash 7-Up

Pour ingredients into shaker with crushed ice. Shake well. Strain into shot glass(es).

PURPLE ALASKAN THUNDER

1 part Jack Daniel's
1 part Southern Comfort
1 part amaretto
1 part Chambord
1 part pineapple juice
1 part sour mix

Pour ingredients into shaker with crushed ice. Shake well. Strain into shot glass(es).

SAMMY SLAMMER

4 parts bourbon
2 parts vanilla liqueur
1 part peach schnapps

Pour directly into shot glass(es).

SHREWSBURY SLAMMER

2 parts bourbon
2 parts peach schnapps
3 parts apple cider

Pour ingredients into shaker with crushed ice. Shake well. Strain into shot glass(es).

SICILIAN KISS

1 part bourbon
1 part amaretto

Pour directly into shot glass(es).

SoCo Kamikaze

5 parts Southern Comfort
3 parts triple sec
4 parts lime juice

Pour directly into shot glass(es).

Southern Blues

1 part Southern Comfort
1 part blueberry schnapps

Pour directly into shot glass(es).

SOUTHERN BONDAGE

1 part Southern Comfort
1 part amaretto
1 part peach schnapps
1 part triple sec
1 splash cranberry juice
1 splash sour mix

Pour ingredients into shaker with crushed ice. Shake well. Strain into shot glass(es).

SOUTHERN PRIDE

2 parts Southern Comfort
1 part peach schnapps

Pour directly into shot glass(es).

SOUTHERN SMILE

1 part Southern Comfort
1 part amaretto
2 parts cranberry juice

Pour ingredients into shaker with crushed ice. Shake well. Strain into shot glass(es).

THREE WISE MEN

1 part Jack Daniel's
1 part Jim Beam
1 part Johnnie Walker

Pour ingredients directly into shot glass(es).

VULCAN MIND PROBE

1 part bourbon
1 part ouzo

Pour directly into shot glass(es).

other
shooters

*When you stop drinking,
you have to deal with this
marvelous personality that started
you drinking in the first place.*

JIMMY BRESLIN

Before you shoot these, know this:

The shots contained in this section are here because they are the outlaws of shooter society. They contain liquors that don't easily fit into the most common bartending  categories (Jägermeister, Bailey's Irish Cream, Rumple Minze), or they combine (equally) way too many of the most common spirits (say, rum, tequila, vodka, and bourbon). Either way, many of these are stronger, more flavorful, and more creative than the previous ones. Further, many of these require additional supplies which you may not have at your immediate disposal (i.e., within an arm's reach of your basic bar): milk, candy, fruit juice, sugar, Red Bull, and other various grocery-store-run-necessary items, plus glassware that is a lot bigger than a 1-1/2-ounce shot glass. Follow the directions carefully. Use the right glasses. We wouldn't lead you astray.

One other thing to keep in mind: The alcohols in the following shooters are sometimes hard to find or uncommon. The recipes require some forethought, some planning, some "tracking down." Let us be the ones to tell you: Do the legwork. Round up the spirits. Hunt down the ingredients. These shooters are worth it.

BUTTERY NIPPLE

1 part butterscotch schnapps
1 part Bailey's Irish Cream

Pour schnapps into shot glass(es). Add Bailey's using a spoon. Do not stir.

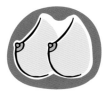

CEMENT MIXER

1 part Bailey's Irish Cream
1 part lime juice

Using two separate shot glasses, pour a half-shot of Bailey's into one and a half-shot of lime juice into the other. Shoot the Bailey's first, and keep the liquor in your mouth. Then, with the Bailey's still in your mouth, shoot the lime juice. Shake your head back and forth, mimicking a cement truck. Swallow the liquid before it fully congeals.

THE CHIQUITA

2 parts vodka
1 part crème de bananes
2 parts milk

Pour ingredients into shaker with crushed ice. Shake well. Strain into shot glass(es).

FLAMING CIDER BOMB

2 parts Hornsby's Cider
1 part Hot Damn
2 Hot Tamales candies

Pour alcohol into shaker with crushed ice. Shake well. Strain into highball glass(es). Add Hot Tamales and let dissolve for a few minutes.

FOUR HORSEMEN

1 part bourbon
1 part scotch
1 part tequila
1 part Jägermeister

Pour ingredients into shaker with crushed ice. Shake well. Strain into shot glass(es).

IRISH CAR BOMB

1/2 pint Guinness
2 parts Jameson
1 part Bailey's Irish Cream

Pour Guinness into pint glass. In a separate shot glass, float Bailey's on top of Jameson. Drop shot glass, carefully, into Guinness half-pint. Drink quickly, lest it curdle.

JÄGER BOMB

1 part Jägermeister
1 part Red Bull

Fill highball glass full of ice. Pour half-full with Red Bull and finish the rest with Jägermeister. Using a straw, suck the drink from the bottom of the glass. Do not mix. Do not pause until the shooter is finished.

LOBOTOMY

1 part Chambord
1 part pineapple juice
1 part amaretto
1 part champagne

Pour Chambord, pineapple juice, and amaretto in a shaker with crushed ice. Strain into shot glass(es). Top with champagne.

LUNCHBOX

1 part citron vodka
1 part rum
1 part Midori melon liqueur
1 part peach schnapps
1 splash pineapple juice
1 splash sour mix
1 splash 7-Up

Pour ingredients into shaker with crushed ice. Shake well. Strain into shot glass(es).

OATMEAL COOKIE

1 part Bailey's Irish Cream
1 part butterscotch schnapps
1 part Grand Marnier

Pour ingredients into shaker with crushed ice. Shake well. Strain into shot glass(es).

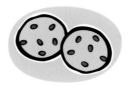

I'd rather have a bottle in front of me than a frontal lobotomy.

TOM WAITS

OATMEAL RAISIN COOKIE

1 part Bacardi 151-proof rum
1 part Bailey's Irish Cream
1 part Goldschläger
1 part Jägermeister
1 part Kahlúa

Pour ingredients into shaker with crushed ice. Shake well. Strain into shot glass(es).

OIL SPILL

1 part Bacardi 151-proof rum
1 drop Kahlúa
1 part Everclear

Pour the Bacardi 151 into shot glass(es); drop Kahlúa in next. Then add the Everclear.

Orgasm

1 part amaretto
1 part Bailey's Irish Cream
1 part Kahlúa

Pour ingredients into shaker with crushed ice. Shake well. Strain into shot glass(es).

When I read about the evils of drinking, I gave up reading.

HENNY YOUNGMAN

PURPLE-HEADED YOGURT SLINGER

2 parts Tequila Rose
1 part blue curaçao
1 part grenadine
1 teaspoon sugar

Pour ingredients into shaker with crushed ice. Shake well. Strain into shot glass(es).

ROCKY MOUNTAIN BEAR PUCKER

1 part Bacardi 151 rum
1 part Jack Daniel's
1 part tequila

Pour ingredients into shaker with crushed ice. Shake well. Strain into shot glass(es).

RUMPLE SHOCK

1 part Rumple Minze
1 part Aftershock

Pour directly into shot glass(es).

RUSTY NAIL

1 part scotch
1 part Drambuie

Pour ingredients into shaker with crushed ice. Shake well. Strain into shot glass(es).

SLIPPERY NIPPLE

1 part sambuca
1 part Bailey's Irish Cream

Pour sambuca directly into shot glass(es). Float Bailey's on top.

SOPHOMORE MIXER

1 part gin
1 part rum
1 part vodka
1 part blue curaçao
1 part grape juice
1 part grapefruit juice
1 part lime juice
1 part sour mix

Pour ingredients into shaker with crushed ice. Shake well. Strain into shot glass(es).

jigglers

*Never accept a drink
from a urologist.*

Erma Bombeck

Jiggler is a generic name for a gelatin shot. (We like Jell-O in our recipes because . . . well, we like Bill Cosby.) Perfect  for parties and festive occasions, these concoctions take some time to make. They need to be refrigerated and hardened for a few hours. They also require special trips to the grocery store for ingredients that you might not have lying around the house. You will need pans, bowls, and two-ounce cups. So, be sure to plan ahead.

Your reward?—a large group of happy friends eating—yes, eating—liquor that they probably can't taste. You'll be the hit of the party. Or the holiday. Or the Tuesday. Whatever the occasion.

(Note: Jell-O packages are in ounces, so we use "ounces," not "parts," in this section. Jiggler recipes assume cups are half filled.)

BATTERY PACK JIGGLERS

16 ounces water
3-ounce package of cranberry Jell-O
3-ounce package of peach Jell-O
8 ounces vodka
8 ounces Red Bull

In a small saucepan bring the water to a boil. Pour boiling water into a medium-sized heatproof bowl and add the cranberry and peach Jell-O. Stir until dissolved. Let cool. Add vodka and Red Bull to cooled mixture. Stir. Pour mixture into thirty 2-ounce cups and refrigerate. Chill 4 to 6 hours.

Buzz-Saw Jigglers

3 ounces espresso or coffee
4 ounces half and half
1 teaspoon chocolate syrup
Dash of ground cinnamon
1 ounce unflavored gelatin
3 ounces vodka
2 ounces Kahlúa
2 ounces crème de cacao

In small saucepan combine espresso, half and half, chocolate syrup, and cinnamon over medium heat. Bring mixture to low boil. Pour heated espresso mixture into a medium-sized heatproof bowl and add gelatin. Stir until dissolved. Let cool. Add vodka, Kahlúa, and crème de cacao to cooled mixture. Stir. Pour mixture into fifteen 2-ounce cups and refrigerate. Chill 4 to 6 hours.

GROG NOG JIGGLERS

8 ounces eggnog
1 ounce unflavored gelatin
5 ounces rum
2 ounces coconut milk
1/2 teaspoon vanilla extract
1 pinch ground cinnamon

In a small saucepan bring eggnog to a low boil. Pour the eggnog into a medium-sized heatproof bowl and add gelatin. Stir until dissolved. Let cool. Add rum, coconut milk, vanilla extract, and cinnamon to cooled mixture. Stir. Pour mixture into fifteen 2-ounce cups and refrigerate. Chill 4 to 6 hours.

"IF LIFE HANDS YOU A LIMON" JIGGLERS

8 ounces water
3-ounce package of cranberry Jell-O
5 ounces vodka
1 ounce Limoncello liqueur
1 ounce lime juice
1 ounce triple sec

In a small saucepan bring the water to a low boil. Pour the boiling water into a medium-sized heatproof bowl and add the cranberry Jell-O. Stir until dissolved. Let cool. Add vodka, Limoncello, lime juice, and triple sec to the cooled mixture. Stir. Pour mixture into fifteen 2-ounce cups and refrigerate. Chill 4 to 6 hours.

JULEP JIGGLERS

8 ounces water
2 small packages unflavored gelatin
8 ounces bourbon
1/2 cup fresh mint leaves, finely chopped
3 tablespoons superfine sugar

In a small saucepan, bring the water to a boil. Pour the boiling water into a medium-sized heatproof bowl and add the unflavored gelatin. Stir until dissolved. Let cool. In a small bowl, mash the bourbon, mint, and sugar with a spoon until the sugar is dissolved. Add to the cooled mixture. Pour mixture into fifteen 2-ounce paper cups and refrigerate. Chill 4 to 6 hours.

LIGHTNING IN A DIXIE CUP JIGGLERS

8 ounces water
3-ounce package of lime Jell-O
4 ounces vodka
3 ounces original Lemon-Lime Gatorade
1 ounce KeKe Beach key lime cream liqueur

In a small saucepan bring water to a low boil. Pour boiling water into a medium-sized heat-proof bowl and add lime Jell-O. Stir until dissolved. Let cool. Add vodka, Gatorade, and key lime liqueur to cooled mixture. Stir. Pour mixture into fifteen 2-ounce cups and refrigerate. Chill 4 to 6 hours.

MARY QUITE CONTRARY JIGGLERS

8 ounces tomato juice
3-ounce package of lemon Jell-O
6 ounces pepper vodka
1 ounce lime juice
1/2 teaspoon wasabi paste
Dash of Worcestershire sauce

In a small saucepan bring tomato juice to a boil. Pour boiling tomato juice into a medium-sized heatproof bowl. Add the lemon Jell-O. Stir until dissolved. Let cool. Add pepper vodka, lime juice, wasabi, and Worcestershire to the cooled mixture. Stir. Pour mixture into fifteen 2-ounce cups and refrigerate. Chill 4 to 6 hours.

PRICKLY CACTI JIGGLERS

6 ounces water
3-ounce package of lime Jell-O
5 ounces tequila
2 ounces triple sec
1 ounce lime juice
1 ounce orange juice

In a small saucepan, bring water to a boil. Pour boiling water into a medium-sized heatproof bowl. Add the Jell-O. Stir until dissolved. Let cool. Add tequila, triple sec, lime juice, and orange juice to the cooled mixture. Stir. Pour the mixture into fifteen 2-ounce cups and refrigerate. Chill 4 to 6 hours.

SWEET MORNING GLORY JIGGLERS

8 ounces water
3-ounce package lime Jell-O
5 ounces white rum
2 ounces fresh grapefruit juice
1 ounce maraschino liqueur

In a small saucepan, bring the water to a boil. Pour the boiling water into a medium-sized heatproof bowl and add the lime Jell-O. Stir until dissolved. Let cool. Add the rum, grapefruit juice, and maraschino liqueur to the cooled mixture. Stir the mixture until well-combined. Pour into fifteen 2-ounce paper cups and refrigerate. Chill 4 to 6 hours.

VERY BERRY JELL-O JIGGLERS

12 ounces boiling water
3-ounce package of Berry Blue Jell-O
4 ounces strawberry schnapps

In a small saucepan, bring the water to a boil. Pour the boiling water into a medium-sized heatproof bowl and add the Jell-O. Stir until dissolved. Let cool. Finally, add the strawberry schnapps to the cooled mixture, stirring until well-combined. Pour into fifteen 2-ounce cups and refrigerate. Chill 4 to 6 hours.

21st birthday adventures

Drink what you want.
Drink what you're able.
If you are drinking with me,
You'll be under the table.

UNKNOWN

No one's 21st birthday is complete without a few shooters. (We're not encouraging; we're just pointing out.) With that in mind, we'd like to offer some easy-to-follow guidelines (etiquette, if you will) to aid those once-in-a-lifetime nights.

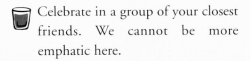 Celebrate in a group of your closest friends. We cannot be more emphatic here.

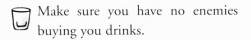 Make sure you have no enemies buying you drinks.

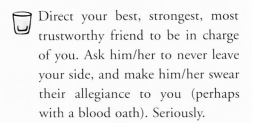 Direct your best, strongest, most trustworthy friend to be in charge of you. Ask him/her to never leave your side, and make him/her swear their allegiance to you (perhaps with a blood oath). Seriously.

Bar hop, when at all possible. Appoint sober drivers, take a cab, or most satisfying—walk from one gin joint to the next. The more places you enter, the more free shooters you will get. Bars have a vested interest in converting the newly legal into lifelong patrons.

 Mix tough-to-take-down shooters with the piece-of-cake ones. This will extend your night.

 Use water as your chaser, not beer.

 Take your time. It's a celebration, not a race. You will earn respect for how long you last, not how quickly you throw up.

If you are the 21st birthday shot buyer, watch out for your friend. You like him enough to celebrate with him, so don't try to send him to the hospital. At the same time, consider the following shooters, most of which fall into the category "Will Put Hair On Your Chest."

- Blow Job (see page 72)
- Dirty Sailor (see page 60)
- Four Horsemen (see page 104)
- Liquid Cocaine (see page 49)
- Lunchbox (see page 107)
- Mind Eraser (see page 77)
- Three Wise Men (see page 99)

bartenders' favorites

*No animal ever invented
anything as bad as drunkenness—
or as good as drink.*

G. K. CHESTERTON

Any good bartender will have a go-to shot—either one that he or she created, or one they like to serve when they get the command:

"Hey, bartender! Round of shots for me and my gang. You call it."

In this section, some of our favorite bartenders from some of our favorite cities provide us with their best shooters.

ATLANTA'S BURNING

Rhett Lynaugh, of Sullivan's Steakhouse in Indianapolis, Indiana, has a name that's always come with pre-conceived notions. "No, I've never heard the *Gone with the Wind* thing before . . . that's funny," he says, his reply drier than vermouth. To combat his would-be annoyers, Rhett has concocted this, his own brand of Northern aggression.

2 parts peach schnapps
1 part Hot Damn
1 part vodka
Dash of 151 rum

Strain first three ingredients into glass. Top with 151. Ignite. (Beware of carpetbaggers.)

CUBBY BLUE

To be honest, Kate Skye's heart is in Boston. But since she's moved to Chicago, where she's a party planner with J² Productions, she's had to at least *appear* to shift loyalties a bit. Stepping behind the bar, she created this concoction in  celebration of her new hometown baseball team. "Hey Chicago," says Skye, "Boston feels your pain. It's the least I can do."

1 part blue curaçao
1 part Bacardi
1 splash grenadine

Pour ingredients directly into shot glass(es).

GREEN THING

Barmeister Chris Paulding of O'Shucks Bar & Grill in Park City, Utah, serves up Green Thing to warm ski bunnies on a cold winter night. Anywhere else in the world, this would be a gargantuan shot, but due to Utah's restrictive liquor laws, this one has to be shared between two or more friends.

2 parts vodka
2 parts tequila
1 part 151 rum
1 part triple sec
1 splash Rose's Lime Juice
1 splash sour mix

Shake over ice and strain into shot glasses.

THE JUICY WATERMELON

Yes, Jeff Tomlinson is a certified master of mixology but, more important, he earned what amounts to a practicum in the art while pouring at bars up and down the East Coast. Brian Boru's Irish Pub in Lake Worth, Florida, is where this New Jersey native now holds court and creates potent drinks such as this.

1 part Bacardi Limón
1 part Watermelon Pucker
1 splash sour mix
1 splash 7-Up

Pour ingredients into shaker with crushed ice. Shake well. Strain into shot glass(es).

OPENING NIGHT

Rick Wesley knows about Opening Nights. He serves them all the time. Wesley is a bartender at Angus McIndoe, the New York landmark nestled right in next to the St. James Theater, and the Opening Night is the bar's signature drink. (FYI: The St. James has been the home of *The Producers* and other enormously popular Broadway shows.) Appropriately, the restaurant/bar really pushes the concoction whenever there actually is an opening night . . . or when a new actor takes over a long-running role . . . or when . . . well, whenever. And according to Wesley, if you pop in at just the right time, you might find yourself sharing happy hour—and an Opening Night—with a Kevin Spacey or a Matthew Broderick or a Brian Dennehy. "Think of the drink as a shooter served in a martini glass," says Wesley.

2 parts Ketel One vodka
1 splash Grand Marnier
1 splash lime juice
1 splash lemon juice
1 splash orange juice
1 drop maple syrup
1 part champagne
2 kisses Chambord

Place vodka, Grand Marnier, juices, and maple syrup into shaker with ice. Strain into chilled martini glass(es) with sugar on the rim. Top with champagne. Then top with two kisses of Chambord.

SANDALS BLUES

Lawrence Herman, now head bartender at Sandals Regency St. Lucia Golf Resort & Spa, was on his second day of employment when he was asked by his boss to participate in a bartenders' competition. "It meant me having to come up with a name and drink in less than five minutes—he was adamant that I do this as quickly as possible." Walking into the competition Herman raised his head and all he could see was the blue sky— not a cloud in sight. "So the perfect name dawned on me: Sandals Blue," he recalls. "And could you believe it, it won first prize." Here's that award-winner, translated into a shooter.

3 parts milk
2 parts crème de bananes
1 part blue curaçao
1 part Kahlúa
3 parts coconut cream

Place all ingredients in shaker with ice. Strain into glasses and, if you have room, garnish with fresh fruit.

THE SUNDOWNER

The Sundowner was created by bar manager Scott Corry of Topper's at The Wauwinet for the neighboring Wauwinet Yacht Club, on Nantucket Island, Massachusetts. (They say the Wauwinet Yacht Club is possibly the oldest in New England, you know. Not sure, of course, who "they" are.) The Sundowner is derivative of a traditional West Indian rum punch, and is intentionally not too sweet, like most rum concoctions you find in the states.

1 part Bacardi Silver
1 part dark rum
1 part light rum
1 part amaretto
1 dash bitters
1 part pineapple juice
1 part orange juice

1 splash cranberry juice ("to give it just a little New England provenance")

Pour ingredients into shaker with crushed ice. Shake well. Strain into shot glass(es). Top with fresh nutmeg and serve with a wedge of lime.

The hard part about being a bartender is figuring out who is drunk and who is just stupid.

RICHARD BRAUNSTEIN

INDEX

Drinks by Name